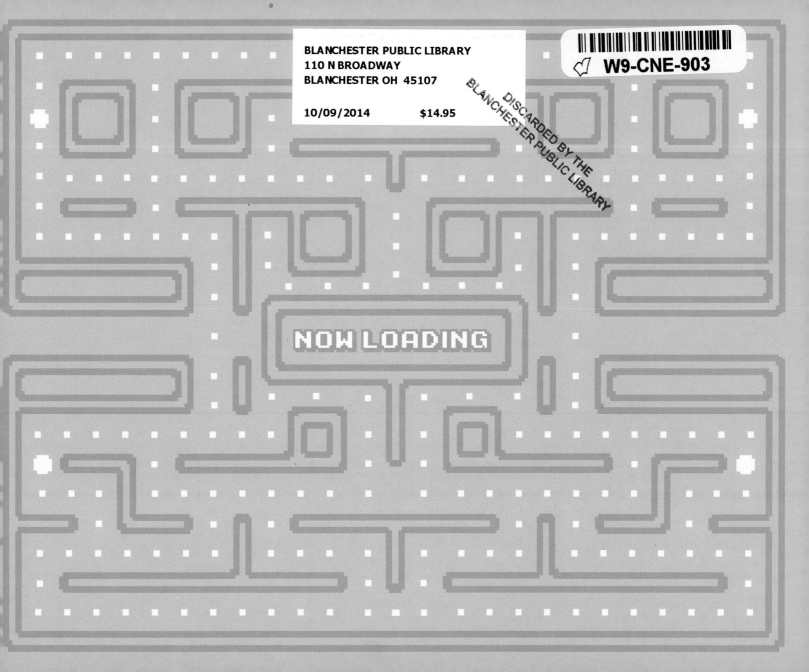

NOW LOADING

ATTACK! BOSS! CHEAT CODE!

ATTACK! BOSS! CHEAT CODE!

A GAMER'S ALPHABET

Chris Barton   Joey Spiotto

POW!
Brooklyn

×14

A IS FOR ATTACK!!!

Hitting certain buttons at the right speed in the right pattern and at just the right time allows the character you control to jump, throw, grab, spin, hammer, slam, swing, fling, flip, or fly.

B IS FOR BOSS

The big, bad leader of the bad guys—the last enemy you've got to beat in battle before you can advance to the next LEVEL or win the whole game.

C IS FOR CHEAT CODE

Cheat codes are tricks (sort of secret, but not really) for making a game easier. Or more fun. Or—as the name suggests—not entirely fair.
For instance, you might know to hit:

Ctrl + Shift + C

then type:

ARMORED-CHIHUAHUA

to make your character stronger. And your opponent might not.

GOLD - MAX: 1,000,000
1,000,000

MAGIC - MAX: 700,000
700,000

LEVEL: 75/75
HEALTH: FULL

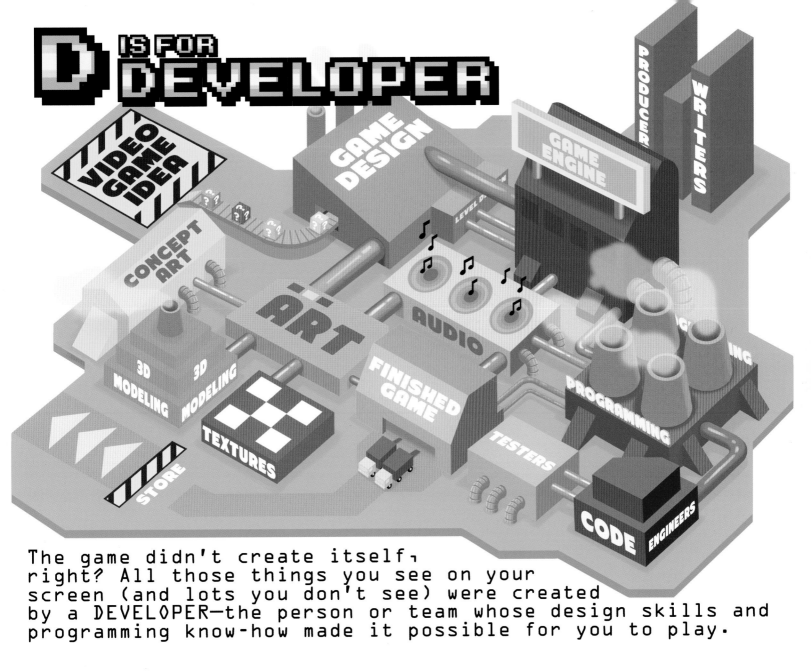

D IS FOR DEVELOPER

The game didn't create itself,
right? All those things you see on your
screen (and lots you don't see) were created
by a DEVELOPER—the person or team whose design skills and
programming know-how made it possible for you to play.

E IS FOR EASTER EGG

Sort of an inside secret joke between the DEVELOPER and you. This could be a word or image or sound or experience— a hidden surprise slipped in for the pleasure of players who stumble into it or know where to look.

F IS FOR FIRST-PERSON

Whatever your character sees, you see. When you observe everything through the eyes of the avatar you control—and neither of you knows what lurks around the next corner or just snuck up behind you—that's FIRST-PERSON.

HELLO. MY NAME IS

MR.VIKING

H4M-BURGER

TTLY-AWESUM

K̶I̶N̶G̶ ̶O̶F̶ ̶T̶H̶E̶ ̶H̶I̶L̶L̶

H IS FOR HANDLE

Xtreme_Machine?
Super_DOOper?
Armored_Chihuahua?

Your HANDLE is the screen
name or alias you use so
that you can keep your
real name private when
playing online.

Private Game: #14

GAME IN PROGRESS

Password: ******

Dungeon: "Middle Realm"

Type: Invitation Only

Population: 20/20 - Full

I IS FOR INSTANCE

When your group is playing an online game, and another group is playing the same game at the same time, you might not want to play together. INSTANCES (sometimes called INSTANCE dungeons) are private areas that either group can enter in order to have the game to itself.

J IS FOR JOYSTICK

A crude device used by ancient civilizations—by your dad, your mom, even your grandparents—to move game avatars around before modern controllers came along.

K IS FOR KART RACING

As all those different sections in the store suggest, there are lots of genres of games. In this cartoony corner of the vehicle racing genre, the goal is simple: reach the finish line faster than the other drivers.

L IS FOR LEVEL

Once you've gotten good at one of these stages—mastered the tasks, pocketed the prizes, beaten the BOSS—you get to LEVEL up and take on new challenges more fitting for your higher rank.

CHECKPOINT CHAMPION

YOU WIN!
1st
MONSTER WHEELS

WINNER'S CUP!

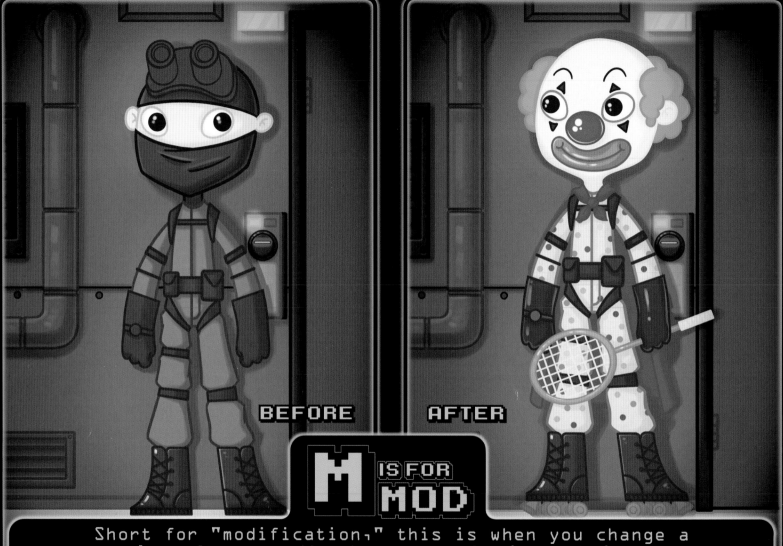

BEFORE

AFTER

M IS FOR MOD

Short for "modification," this is when you change a
game's software or hardware to make it work in a way
the original DEVELOPER didn't have in mind. It's entirely
possible for you and your friends to spend more time
installing MODS together than actually playing.

 **IS FOR N00B**

NEWBIE > NOOB > N00B

See how numbers replaced those letters?
That demonstrates a kind of gaming lingo
called leetspeak (or l33t speak, or
1337 speak, or just 1337).

Of 411 7h3 3x4mpl35 0u7 7h3r3, n00b
—f0r 0bv10u5 r3450n5—m4y b3 7h3
f1r57 0n3 y0u run 1n70.*

*Of all the examples out there, n00b—for obvious reasons
—may be the first one you run into.

O IS FOR OPEN BETA

Before Armored Chihuahua 3 is ready to be sold, DEVELOPERS need players to try it out and suggest improvements. That test period is called a beta—it may be closed at first to all but a chosen few, but then opened up to lots of people to find as many fixes as possible.

P IS FOR

POWER-UP

A bigger size, a different form, an awesome new ability—these are the sorts of benefits your character gets(usually only for a little while) from collecting POWER-UPs.

Q is for Quest

Just like an action-packed book or adventure movie, some types of games have a plot where you're on a QUEST —a series of challenges you must overcome if you want to reach a goal that's important to you.

Start

SELECT YOUR
HERO!!!

CLASS :

WARRIOR

HEALTH: ___500
STRENGTH: ___300
SPEED: ___250
ARMOR: ___175
MAGIC: ___100

CHARACTER TYPE :

ELF ☐☐☐☐☐☐☐☐☐

BACK  NEXT

 **IS FOR** **RPG** Short for Role-Playing Game, and part
of a longer acronym (MMORPG, for
Massively Multiplayer Online Role-Playing Game). Filled
with QUESTS, characters, strategies, and interactions,
these are best played with people you like, because you
could be at it for a long, long time.

S IS FOR SANDBOX

Sometimes, you just want the freedom to mine, or build, or explore in an open world rather than stick to a QUEST. Sandbox is a type of game or style of play where you can make it up as you go.

T IS FOR THIRD-PERSON

X140

Unlike FIRST-PERSON, in THIRD-PERSON you see your avatar from the outside— you're still in control, but you watch your character just like you do your allies and enemies.

YOU'VE UNLOCKED:

SPEED:
SHIELD:
HANDLING:

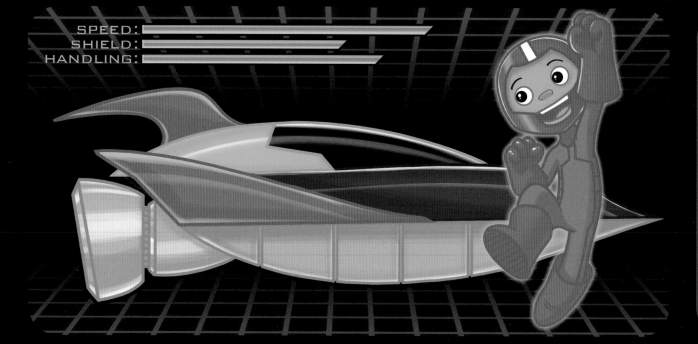

X-BLASTER 5000

 **PREV** **NEXT** **U** IS FOR

UNLOCKABLE

Some parts of a game—certain characters, minigames, modes of play, and whatnot—aren't available at the very beginning, but you're able to unlock them after getting past various obstacles. Or, you know, after entering

V IS FOR VECTOR

Video games have been around for a long time
(see: JOYSTICK), and they've used different kinds of graphics
over the years. Many early arcade games were done in
VECTORS—the lines (line segments, technically) connecting
two points. VECTOR games' sharp images and smooth moves
showed how much you could do with just points, lines,
circles, and curves.

▶ 🔊 01.33 / 12.00   🕐 ⚏ ⚙ ▭ ⌜⌟

W is for Walkthrough

😊   Armored_Chihuahua   123 videos   **182, 541**

▶ Subscribe ⟨ 1,043, 210 ⟩   👍 33,071   👎 19

👍 Like 👎   About   Share   Add to   🖶   ㆔   ⚑

If you need a little guidance to help you get better at a game, WALKTHROUGHS can be your friends. But if the few minutes you meant to spend watching useful tips from other players turns into an hour spent zoned out without actually playing, maybe not so much.

Top comments ⌄

X IS FOR XP

And what does XP stand for? Experience Points. As you defeat BOSSES or complete QUESTS, you pick up XP—a measurement of your progress toward your next chance to LEVEL up.

You Earned:

500XP

Y IS FOR
YOKE

No, this is not what you find in the EASTER EGG. Some games need their own special hardware. For flight simulators, it's a YOKE—the thing that controls a plane, which will make you feel much more like an actual pilot in an actual cockpit.

Z IS FOR

ZERG

Some opponents are too big
and strong to take on by yourself,
so what can you do? ZERG'em—gang up
with a bunch of other smaller, weaker
characters to swarm the enemy side and

SO, THE NEXT TIME YOU HEAR...

"This **open beta** game is in **third-person** but **first-person** is **unlockable** if you know the **cheat code** or install this **mod**, but either way, for the best **attack** on the **boss** on this **level**, try to grab that **power-up**—if you can't, a guy in a **walkthrough** showed how you can advance by plugging in a **yoke**, but then you won't get to see the **developer**'s cool **Easter egg** that turns the whole game into armored-chihuahua **kart racing** for a few seconds —or instead we could play this new **RPG** that's the greatest thing since **vectors** and **joysticks**, if you can find an **instance** where there aren't any **griefers** trying to disrupt your **quest** and there are other **n00bs** to help you **zerg** the enemy while you rack up **XP**, unless you'd rather just play in **sandbox** mode.

Either way, what do you want for your **handle**?"

Attack! Boss! Cheat Code!
A Gamer's Alphabet

Published in the United States by POW!
a division of powerHouse Packaging & Supply, Inc.

Text © 2014 Chris Barton
To Ty Russell, for all the fun and games (onscreen and off)

Illustrations © 2014 Joey Spiotto
For my Mom and Dad, for always supporting my passions for drawing and video games

ISBN 978-1-57687-701-2

Library of Congress Control Number: 2014937058

powerHouse Packaging & Supply, Inc.
37 Main Street, Brooklyn, NY 11201-1021

info@bookpow.com
www.bookpow.com
www.powerHousebooks.com
www.powerHousepackaging.com

First edition, 2014

Book design by Joey Spiotto

10 9 8 7 6 5 4 3 2 1

Printed in Malaysia

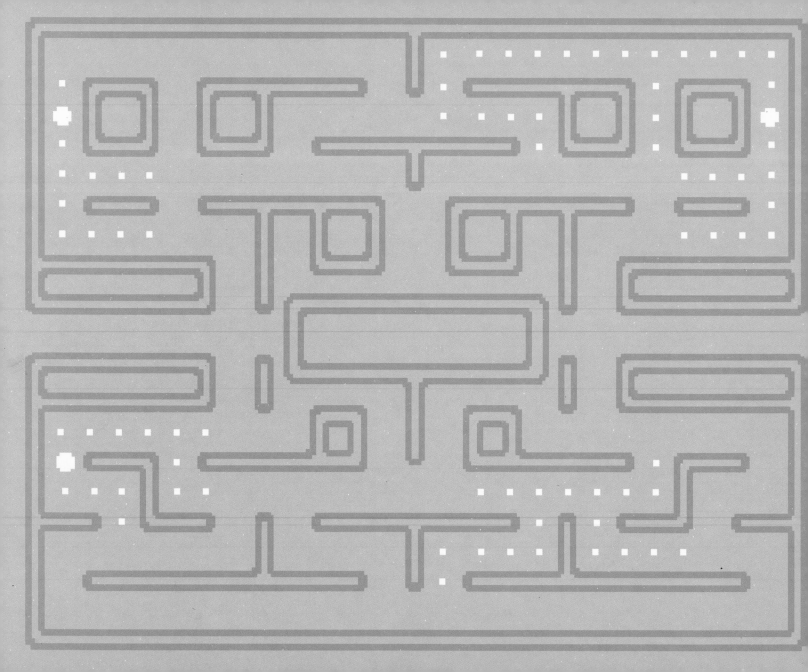